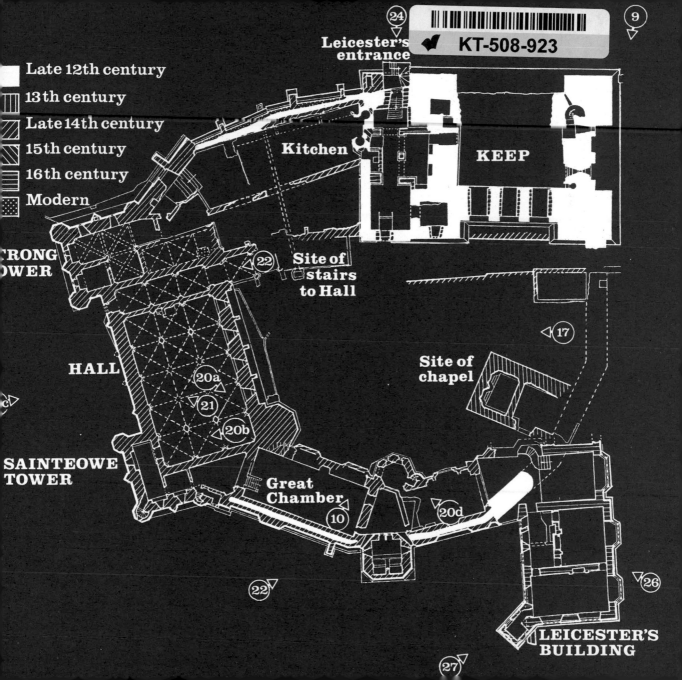

Late 12th century
13th century
Late 14th century
15th century
16th century
Modern

Leicester's
entrance

Kitchen

KEEP

STRONG
TOWER

22

Site of
stairs
to Hall

17

HALL

Site of
chapel

20a

21

20b

SAINTEOWE
TOWER

Great
Chamber

10

20d

22

26

27

LEICESTER'S
BUILDING

24

9

KENILWORTH CASTLE

D. F. RENN

**DEPARTMENT OF
THE ENVIRONMENT**

HER MAJESTY'S STATIONERY OFFICE LONDON 1973

Crown Copyright

Crown Copyright

CONTENTS

FRONTISPIECE: *This dramatic engraving of the ruined Norman keep, illuminated by a flash of lightning, brilliantly evokes the grandeur of its dominating position in the castle.*

TITLE PAGE: *An elaborate fireplace in Leicester's Gatehouse has his initials, his motto and his badge carved in stone, with Gothic details on each side of the opening. The wooden overmantel, with its free-standing columns, does not fit the stonework below.*

OPPOSITE: *The Great Hall in the early nineteenth century, overgrown and grazed by sheep. Notice the scale of the windows, and compare with the photographs on pages 20 and 21.*
These three illustrations are from Kenilworth Illustrated, published by Merridew and Son, Coventry and Warwick, 1821.

ABOVE: *Engraving of the castle by Samuel and Nathaniel Buck, published in 1729.*

Designed by Peter Forster
of the Directorate of Information
Department of the Environment

5

Printed in England for Her Majesty's Stationery Office by Westerham Press Limited   Dd 503923 K400 3/73

Midland England has but few really magnificent castles, and Kenilworth has lost what was once its most striking feature: the great lake, half a mile long and up to a quarter of a mile wide, which surrounded the castle and formed its water defences. But it is still one of the grandest ruined castles in the kingdom, and the mellow red sandstone has blended together the work of the different centuries in a wonderful harmony. The first fortress of earth and timber, ditch and palisaded bank, was rebuilt in stone in the late twelfth century. King John added an outer court with towers built at strategic intervals. John of Gaunt remodelled the domestic buildings, Henry V built a banqueting house on the other side of the lake, and yet more buildings were added in Tudor days, when Queen Elizabeth I was entertained here, regardless of expense, by her favourite, Robert Dudley, Earl of Leicester.

Much of Warwickshire's countryside is well forested, with low rounded hills and broad valleys produced by the erosion of the New Red Sandstone over the ages. Kenilworth stands on a knoll of rock and gravel, naturally protected by marshes, at the junction of the Finham and Inchford Brooks. Right from the beginning these natural fortifications were utilized and improved by damming the streams south of the site of the castle in order to produce a wide 'moat' surrounding the island on which the castle stood.

The best way to understand how and why the building of Kenilworth Castle developed as it did, is first of all to go round the inner court anti-clockwise, beginning with the great keep – the tallest building, without windows

OPPOSITE: *A reconstruction of the castle c.1575, by Alan Sorrell. In the foreground is Leicester's Gatehouse, flanked by Lunn's Tower (left) and the Swan Tower (right). Behind the Tudor garden is the inner court, with the Norman keep in front of Leicester's Buildings and the Great Hall and Chambers to their right. Beyond is the great lake and (top left) the Brays earthwork.*

ABOVE: *Wood engraving of the oriel windows of the inner court, from William Beattie's* Castles and Abbeys in England, *showing the stone panelling of the recesses.*

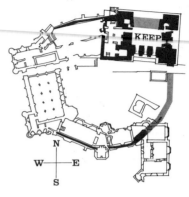

stables, and, last of all, on the way back to the car park, to visit the medieval gatehouse, the Tiltyard and the outer works beyond the dam which once held back one of the largest artificial sheets of water in England. This is the sequence followed by the rest of this guidebook.

LEFT: *Kenilworth Castle from the air, looking eastward. The low wall flanking the great lake is in the foreground, and behind it is the outer facade of the Great Hall. The Norman keep is in the middle of the photograph; Leicester's Buildings can be seen on each side of it. The stables in the background are partly concealed by trees.*

ABOVE: *The keep from the north-east, showing two of the massive corner turrets. Part of the interior can be seen where the north wall has fallen away.*

NEXT PAGE: *The keep from the south, looking across the inner court from the site of the Great Chamber. The doorway on the left leads into the forebuilding which contained a staircase to the main entrance to the keep itself. Most of the windows were altered for the Earl of Leicester in the sixteenth century.*

THE NORMAN KEEP

King Henry I gave the royal manor of Stoneleigh, of which Kenilworth formed a part, to his chamberlain Geoffrey de Clinton about fifty years after the Norman Conquest. Geoffrey founded a priory at Kenilworth, which later became an abbey, and allowed the monks to fish on Thursdays with boats and nets in the waters beside his new castle and park. A castle provided some defence for a manor against powerful but acquisitive neighbours (Warwick, with its castle founded by William the Conqueror, was only five miles away) and also a centre for administration. Although Kenilworth is a very pleasant place, Geoffrey de Clinton can have lived here for only short periods, since his duties made it necessary for him to accompany the king much of the time, and the castle was more often occupied by a steward with a constable and a small 'peacetime' garrison.

The buildings of the first castle stood inside a roughly circular embanked enclosure about 200 feet across which was surrounded by a wide flat-bottomed ditch. This ditch has been filled in, although a short section can be seen near the keep. There it has been cleared out to display the stone abutments once spanned by a drawbridge. The solid mass of earth which forms the core of the stone keep may have been a mound or *motte* carrying a timber watch-tower. Naturally all these timber buildings have now vanished.

Later in the twelfth century the defences were rebuilt in stone. The earth bank was replaced by a stone curtain wall and a great keep. The curtain wall has been destroyed to its foundations, but one side of the entrance archway survives, abutting against the angle of the keep; the vertical groove in it was where the portcullis grate rose and fell. The keep was the inner citadel of the castle, designed to resist all forms of attack known in the days before gunpowder. Notice the high sloping plinth covering the lower part of the walls; besiegers would have to bore through a great thickness of stonework, and rams would make little impression either. By spreading the weight of the keep over wide foundations, the builders also hoped that any tunnels cut by attackers would fail to make the tower fall down.

Moving round the keep, we come to the forebuilding door. The forebuilding protected the door of the main keep itself, and provided extra room. In Tudor times the Kenilworth forebuilding was gutted and converted into a court-yard giving access to a pleasure garden between the inner castle and the village. Some of the houses opposite the castle, on Castle Green, have been there since Tudor times. If you stand inside the forebuilding and look to-wards the main keep, you can see the original inner doorway high up to the right. The doorway was approached by a staircase of two flights, and gave access to the upper floor of the keep. Each of the two floors consisted of a single room, and a spiral staircase linked them. Most of the windows have been widened, but one Norman round-topped window remains unaltered. It is a narrow slit, with its sides splaying both inside and outside. Next to it is the well, with a shaft above so that water could be drawn off at either level. In the opposite corner turret is a deep latrine pit – not a dungeon. Each of the corner turrets has a room at a high level, above the roof of the rest of the keep. A wall-walk running right round the parapet above the roof enabled the defenders to overlook all sides of the keep and the rest of the castle.

The keep is the main surviving part of the Norman castle at Kenilworth. When Henry I died, the dispute between Stephen and Matilda over the crown led to nearly twenty years of civil war. Henry II, Matilda's son, was anxious to avoid any repetition of this after his own death and so he had his son – also called Henry – crowned in his own lifetime. But the 'Young King', was not content with glory without power, and rebelled against his father in the year 1173. King Henry the elder took Kenilworth and Warwick castles – among many others – into his own hands, and garrisoned and provisioned them against attack by the supporters of the 'Young King'. King Henry did not return Kenilworth to the Clinton family after the rebellion had ended, but gave them other lands instead, with a very small castle, in Buckinghamshire.

11

A. F. Kersting

King John had extensive improvements made to Kenilworth, including the walling of the outer court (see page 37). The descendant of the Clintons, probably still smarting from the unfair 'bargain' of Henry II, was among the baronial rebels in the civil war at the end of John's reign. Kenilworth was one of the four castles which were to be handed over to the barons as a guarantee of John's performance of Magna Carta, but the king seems to have managed to avoid surrendering it. The clause in the Charter which provided that castles unjustly seized were to be returned seems to have remained a dead letter – certainly in the case of Kenilworth.

Henry III did not often visit Kenilworth, but nevertheless made a characteristic order in 1241 for improvements to be made to the royal apartments. The chapel (perhaps the one whose foundations can be seen near the keep) was to be refitted and decorated, the king's chamber was to be re-roofed, the queen's chamber was to be wainscotted, its windows enlarged and an entrance porch erected. The two gates of the castle were to be repaired and part of the southern wall, which was likely to fall into the fishpond, was to be taken down and rebuilt.

SIEGE OF KENILWORTH

Henry III made a bad mistake when he allowed Simon de Montfort, Earl of Leicester, to marry his sister Eleanor. The king granted them Kenilworth Castle for life, but Simon became the leader of the baronial opposition to the king. While he was in control of the kingdom between 1262 and 1265, Simon based his power on Kenilworth. After the Battle of Lewes in 1264, Henry III's son, the Lord Edward, and the king's brother Richard, Earl of Cornwall, were imprisoned here. Edward was removed to Hereford, but he managed to escape and to raise an army in Worcestershire. De Montfort's younger son – also called Simon – advanced from London to do battle. He and his forces camped outside Kenilworth Castle, because there was insufficient room within. No scouting parties were sent out, since the Lord Edward's army was thought to be thirty miles away. But Edward had a very good intelligence system, and he marched on Kenilworth by night. Edward fell on de Montfort's camp at dawn, killing and capturing many in their beds. Simon

ABOVE: *Funerary effigy of King John, carved in Purbeck marble. The smaller head is that of an attendant bishop, and the whole monument is in Worcester Cathedral.*

RIGHT: *Funerary effigy of Henry III, cast in latten by William Torel, in Edward the Confessor's chapel at Westminster Abbey.*

FAR RIGHT: *Simon de Montfort, as represented in a stained glass window in Chartres Cathedral.*
These three portraits are in different media, but each is a brilliantly successful work of thirteenth-century art.

de Montfort and a few others managed to escape into the castle by swimming the great lake. Three days later, on 4th August, 1265, Edward won the Battle of Evesham at which the elder Simon de Montfort was killed. The younger Simon thereupon released Richard of Cornwall as a gesture of peace, and reached a compromise with Henry III. But Simon's garrison at Kenilworth, strengthened by a local mob, would not accept the agreement; knowing that the castle was well stocked with food and arms, they claimed that they held the castle for the countess Eleanor.

The royal forces moved inexorably upon Kenilworth Castle at Easter, 1266. Henry III offered reasonable terms for surrender but the garrison refused, and broke the rules of war by cutting off the hand of the royal envoy before sending him back. The king arrived in person, and his camp was set up on Castle Green, where the village now stands. The Sword of State 'Curtana' was brought up and displayed in the royal pavilion. The Archbishop of Canterbury solemnly excommunicated the garrison. The garrison, undismayed, replied by dressing up their surgeon, Philip Porpeis, in ecclesiastical-looking clothes, and Philip then mounted the battlements and 'excommunicated' king, archbishop and all their following. Boats were brought overland from Chester for a water-borne assault across the great lake, which was beaten off. A great tower – nicknamed 'The Bear' – was built

1 The woods in y chase
2 The poole
3 The plesance
4 The Swan tower
5 The wall towards the poole
6 The Strong tower archt y stories with stone
7 The Hall
8 Lancasters buildings
9 Cesars Tower

The Prospect of Kenilworth Castle from the old parke, on the South side thereof,

LEFT: *Miniature Norman font, or candlestick, dug up in the grounds of the castle. The lower part is carved like the base of a column, with grotesque heads at the top.*

BELOW: *An early seventeenth-century engraving by Wencelaus Hollar, looking northwards towards Kenilworth Castle across the great lake. On the extreme left are "The woods in ye chase". The main block of buildings in the centre are those surrounding the inner court: from left to right the keep, Great Hall and Chambers, and Leicester's Buildings, with his gatehouse just showing beyond as twin towers. Mortimer's Tower and the Tiltyard are on the right, with the spire of Kenilworth church showing above the skyline.*

RIGHT: *Gold signet ring found in the castle, with an impression of the seal. The date was probably (14)87.*

to give the royal archers a good vantage-point from which to overlook the castle walls. The archers hoped to pick off the engineers working the defenders' catapults, but the catapults won, and slew the 'Bear'. Many of the stone balls which can be seen lying about the castle grounds (particularly in the garden near the keep) are relics of that siege of seven hundred years ago.

The strongest castle will eventually surrender for one reason or another if the attackers are sufficiently persistent. The siege of Kenilworth lasted almost nine months, and moderate counsels eventually prevailed in the royal camp. A great council was held at Coventry, and lenient terms for surrender were again offered to the defenders of the castle. The terms were proclaimed in the royal camp and formally ratified in Warwick church, but they were at first rejected by the garrison. Henry III ordered up further forces of workmen to prepare for a storming of the castle. But before the assault could be mounted, epidemic disease broke out inside the castle, and the garrison surrendered just before Christmas. They were allowed to depart with their arms, horses and harness. There was only two days' food left in the castle.

The north wall of the keep was blown up after the Civil War, so that there is now a good view from here across the pleasure garden to the Tudor and later houses occupying the site of the camp of Henry III.

FROM CASTLE TO PALACE

After the surrender of Kenilworth in 1266, Henry III gave it to his second son Edmund, whom he created Earl of Lancaster. Edmund's son Thomas built a chapel here, perhaps that in the outer court, but he was executed for rebellion against Edward II in 1322. Thomas's brother Henry was made earl in 1324, and two years later Edward II found himself Henry's prisoner at Kenilworth. Forced to sign his abdication here, the king was hurried to Berkeley Castle and to his death. Henry of Lancaster's grand-daughter married John of Gaunt (Ghent), the fourth son of Edward III and fifth Earl of Lancaster.

John of Gaunt spent much of his time at Kenilworth Castle, and he rebuilt the accommodation of the inner court, except for the keep. In 1379 orders were given for forty small oak trees to be used for the repair of the floor of the great chamber 'for dancing on at Christmas', but most of the buildings seem to have been put up between 1389 and 1394. The new accommodation was palatial. A large kitchen was laid out next to the keep forebuilding with a paved floor. The large fireplaces against the old walls were lined with thin tiles set on edge, so that the heat of the fire would not cause them to flake away. After being cooked in the kitchen, the food was carried up a service stair (on the line of the present wooden staircase) to a servery at the level of the Great Hall, where the food was made ready for serving. This servery

National Monuments Record

16

LEFT: *Part of the funerary effigy of Edward II with its beautiful canopy, in Gloucester Cathedral. Notice the angel supporting the king's head.*

RIGHT: *The Great Hall seen from across the inner court. The narrow slits lighting the basement contrast sharply with the great windows above of the hall itself. The entrance stair is on the right, and the oriel window projection on the left.*

BELOW: *The magnificent painting of Henry V, now in the National Portrait Gallery, London.*

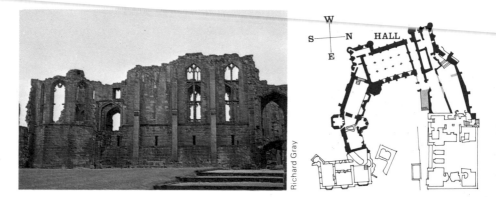

Richard Gray

National Portrait Gallery

formed part of a wing called the Strong Tower, vaulted on each of three floors, the lowest being for storage and the topmost for apartments.

By continuing up the stairs, the visitor can obtain a good view of the whole castle. Looking outwards, across the peaceful fields, it is difficult to visualize them as having been under water during the Middle Ages, and to imagine a great lake lapping against the outer wall below and stretching away for half a mile. There were two small gateways in the outer wall on this side, near one of which was a boathouse for the king's barge.

Henry V found the new Kenilworth buildings too public for his liking, so he had a pavilion (or pleasure-house) built at the far end of the great lake from the rest of the castle, which he called the Pleasaunce in the Marsh (*"Le Pleasaunz en Mares"*). Thomas Elmham, who was present at the Battle of Agincourt and may have written the anonymous account of the battle which has come down to us, wrote a metrical biography of Henry V which describes the king's work at Kenilworth in 1414 thus: *"There was there a fox-ridden place, overgrown with briars and thorns. He removes these and cleanses the site so that wild animals are driven off . . . the coarse ground is sweetened with running water."*

17

ABOVE: *The Pleasaunce from the air. Henry V's private pavilion is situated half a mile to the west of the castle buildings. The two moats, once filled with water, surrounded the courtyard and were linked to the great lake (now drained) by a channel which is just visible (in front of the large tree in the background).*

RIGHT: *Merridew's engraving of the main entrance doorway to John of Gaunt's Great Hall in the castle, showing the delicately-carved details surrounding the inner door frame, with one of the enormous hall windows beyond.*

The site of the Pleasaunce is hidden from most of the castle by a fold in the ground, although a watcher on top of the keep could just see it. The pavilion was timber-framed, and stood in a diamond-shaped courtyard with small square towers at the corners. The walled courtyard was surrounded in turn by two concentric water-filled moats, and was approached from the lake by a wide channel, up which the royal barge could be sailed or rowed almost to the door of the pavilion. The Pleasaunce was kept up by Henry VI and Edward IV, but was demolished by Henry VIII, who had the buildings re-erected in a Pleasaunce of his own, between the inner and outer walls near the Strong Tower.

The Strong Tower is balanced by the Saint Lowe Tower at the other end of the Great Hall, both towers projecting outward to form a symmetrical front to the whole group, which was a very unusual architectural composition for the time. John of Gaunt's Great Hall itself is still a magnificent building, even in ruin. The vaulting which formed both the roof of the basement and the floor of the main hall above it has collapsed, but many of the clustered pillars which once supported the vault still remain against the side walls, and the foundations of others can be seen in the turf. Before the vaulting fell, the basement must have been very dark, the only light coming in through the narrow sloping loops facing the courtyard. Evidently the basement was intended for storage purposes and not for occupation. A passage connecting the inner and outer courts runs through the end bay of the basement nearest the Strong Tower. It could be closed by a portcullis, which was raised or lowered by a rope or chain running through a hole in the window-sill of the hall above the passage.

The lofty windows of the hall itself still have much left of their fine carved stonework, both panelling and tracery, and the two fireplaces have much carving left too. It is a sad fact that as recently as 1842 the tracery of two of the windows of the Great Hall was destroyed by a gentleman *"who said the Castle lookt better as a Ruin"*. When it was first put up, the roof of the Great Hall spanned a greater distance than any other in England, but it was eclipsed a few years later by the new roof of Westminster Hall in London. The carved details of the porch at the top of the former entrance staircase to the Great Hall are very fine – notice in particular the sculptured foliage. A graceful three-sided oriel at the other end of the hall balances the porch. It was designed to give the lord some privacy (and some protection from draughts); it has its own fireplace and gives a good view overlooking the inner court.

18

The late fourteenth-century windows of the Great Hall are among the most magnificent of any in England. FAR LEFT: *One window glimpsed through another in the oriel.* ABOVE LEFT: *One of the best preserved windows, complete with its stone tracery, seen from inside the hall, with the entrance to the Saint Lowe Tower on the left.* ABOVE RIGHT: *The same window can be seen on the extreme left, with the oriel in the foreground.* LEFT: *The hall windows from outside the inner court, and* RIGHT: *Three of the same windows from within. Notice the stone panelling and seats in the recesses.*

The base of the oriel contains a little bit of the earlier hall building, including a window best seen from inside the Great Chamber which adjoins the Great Hall to the south. This chamber and the one beyond it have been much altered and ruined; they formed the state apartments of the castle of John of Gaunt's day, and had large bay windows looking into the courtyard, on each side of another projecting oriel. This oriel lit a lobby between the two chambers, and on the outside of the court is a three-storey block, still standing, which contained garderobes.

The rectangular stone foundations in the inner court, between this oriel and the great keep, once carried a wooden chapel, probably built in the thirteenth century. Other timber-framed buildings with glazed windows were built between this chapel and the keep by order of Henry VIII, some of the

glass being painted with the Royal Arms or the king's badge. These wooden ranges of buildings were extended with stone work in Tudor times, and here is a convenient place to pause and look at the improvements which converted John of Gaunt's palace into a Tudor one.

FAR LEFT: *Ornamented buttress on south side of the Great Chamber, supporting a triangular projection, possibly a window.*

LEFT: *The vaulting between the basement and Great Hall above it has collapsed, leaving only the rough edges and the broken-off pillars against the walls. The door on the right leads to the great lake, and had its own portcullis.*

RIGHT: *The western façade of Kenilworth, from the dry bed of the former lake, which lapped the wall in the foreground. Behind it, the Norman keep on the left and the traceried windows of the Great Hall on the right, flanked by the Strong Tower (centre) and the Saint Lowe Tower (far right).*

FAR LEFT: *Leicester's Gatehouse, seen from high above the inner court of the castle. After the Civil War, Colonel Hawkesworth converted the gatehouse into a dwelling, adding the gabled wing and chimneys visible on the right.*

LEFT CENTRE: *The Tudor porch to the gatehouse (hidden by the tree in the other picture). The doorway has a curiously ribbed underside, and RD (for Robert Dudley) is carved above it. The battlements are for show, not for use, and overlook the great garden.*

RIGHT: *Robert Dudley, created Earl of Leicester in 1564 by Queen Elizabeth I. He was the heir of the Duke of Northumberland, who had been executed by Queen Mary in 1553 soon after he had obtained Kenilworth Castle by exchange. After turning the medieval fortress into a Tudor palace, Robert Dudley often entertained his Queen here until his death in the fateful year of the Armada (1588).*

TUDOR KENILWORTH

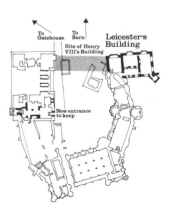

After the Dissolution of the Monasteries, the site of Kenilworth Abbey, near the parish church north and east of the castle, was granted to John Dudley, Duke of Northumberland. After the death of Henry VIII, the crown went to Henry's son Edward, who was not yet in his teens. By 1551 John Dudley had become the virtual ruler of England, but his triumph was to be short-lived. Early in 1553 he obtained Kenilworth Castle and, when the boy-king died later in that year, Dudley attempted to put his own daughter-in-law, Jane Grey, on the throne. But, within a fortnight, a popular rising had transferred the crown to Henry VIII's daughter, Mary Tudor. John Dudley's head lay beside the executioner's block in the Tower of London.

Dudley's eldest son was executed at the same time, but his youngest son, Robert, was to regain Kenilworth ten years later, in 1563. For the reign of Mary was even shorter than that of Edward VI, and handsome young Robert

LEFT: *The east side of Leicester's Buildings as seen from the Base Court. The small rectangular many-paned windows are set in shallow projecting oriels. The indented "toothing" on the far right was to link the Buildings with the earlier range put up by Henry VIII but later destroyed.*

BELOW: *Engraving by Wenceslaus Hollar of the castle from the east, as it appeared in the early seventeenth century. The Tiltyard wall is to the left, with Mortimer's Tower below the tall tree. Leicester's Buildings are on the left of the main block of masonry, with the Norman Keep ("Caesar's Tower") to its right, with Leicester's Gatehouse immediately in front of it.*

RIGHT: *Leicester's Buildings from the south-west, with its projecting tall turret. Notice how thin the walls are for their height.*

KENILWORTH CASTLE

CORRECTION

The text at the top of page 9 should begin

at ground level. Then, to look at the outer
court containing the Tudor gatehouse and

Department of the Environment

July 1973

LONDON: HER MAJESTY'S STATIONERY OFFICE

Dudley was soon high in the favour of the new Queen, Elizabeth I. So high in favour in fact that it was widely rumoured that the two might marry, especially after the mysterious – but convenient – death of Robert Dudley's wife, Amy Robsart, at her house at Cumnor in Berkshire. But passions cooled with time, and Elizabeth's head ruled her heart. Robert Dudley had to content himself with the earldom of Leicester – and with Kenilworth Castle.

Dudley modernized the keep by widening the narrow Norman openings and putting in large square-topped windows. He opened out the forebuilding to form a little forecourt leading to a great pleasure-garden outside the inner court. Beyond the pleasure-garden he built a great gatehouse in typical Tudor style, four-square with octagonal turrets at the corners and many tall mullioned windows like those he had fitted into the Norman keep. This gatehouse replaced the old postern gateway which, like the rest of the outer curtain wall on this side of the castle, has been demolished down to its foundations. The Earl of Leicester intended to make his new gatehouse the centre of a new show-front to the castle, a great façade designed to impress distinguished visitors returning from hunting in the park. After the Civil War, a group of Parliamentary officers bought the castle and one, Colonel Hawkesworth, converted the gatehouse into a private dwelling for himself, blocking up the old entrance gateway and adding the gabled wing on one side.

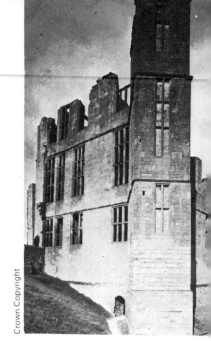

The Prospect thereof vpon the road from Coventre towards Warwick, being the East side,

1 The Gallery-tower
2 The woods in the chase.
3 The outer wall of the Castle towards the poole
4 The Castle mills,
5 Mortimer Tower
6 Leicesters building.
7 Kings Henry the 8 lodginge.
8 Cesars Tower,
9 The Swan-Tower,
10 The roofe of the Stable
11 The great gate-house
12 Lunns Tower.

27

Beyond the screen of trees are great Tudor stables (page 38). To the south of the keep, Robert Dudley extended Henry VIII's timber lodgings with a range of stone buildings. The 'toothed' ends of the walls show that he intended to rebuild the wooden range in stone as well. Much of the stone was second-hand, reworked from the materials of the demolished Kenilworth Abbey. The Tudor windows were in projecting bays, and the walls are very high and thin. It is remarkable how much of this range of buildings still stands, particularly since it was occupied in the eighteenth century by a group of weavers from Coventry, who knocked holes in the walls for their looms and other machinery.

QUEEN ELIZABETH AT KENILWORTH

RIGHT: *Queen Elizabeth I, possibly by Nicholas Hilliard c.1575–80 (Walker Art Gallery, Liverpool).*

ON THE FOLLOWING PAGES: ABOVE: *Wenceslaus Hollar's engraving of a drawing of Kenilworth Castle from the road from Coventry to Warwick (near the present-car park). Leicester's Buildings and the keep are in the middle, with Mortimer's Tower among the trees in front and Leicester's Gatehouse and Lunn's Tower on the far right. BELOW: Queen Elizabeth I on a Royal Progress, from a drawing of Nonsuch Palace by George Houfragel, 1562.*

The Queen and Robert Dudley remained friends, and she often visited him in his new up-to-date palace. The most famous visit was in July 1575, when the Queen was entertained for nineteen days at enormous expense. George Gascoigne was a poet in the Queen's retinue at the time, and he wrote a detailed account of the festivities, which he called *"The Princely Pleasures at the Castle of Kenelwoorthe"*. On her arrival at the castle the Queen was greeted by the Lady of the Lake who stood, surrounded by nymphs, on a floating island. *"Her Majesty,"* says Gascoigne, *"proceeding toward the inward Court, passed on a bridge, the which was rayled on both sides. And in the toppes of the postes thereof were set sundrie presents: as wine, corne, frutes, fishes, fowls, instruments of musike and weapons for martial defence. All which were expounded by an Actor, clad like a Poet . . . This speech being ended, she*

Walker Art Gallery, Liverpool

28

The gallery tower
The woods in the Chase
The tilt-yard wall.

4 The Cottages on Bull hill
5 Mortimers Tower
6 The roofe of the Stable

The prospect thereof vpon
Colshill towards Warwick,

all neere the road from
the North-east side.

7 Leicesters buildings
8 Luns Tower
9 Cæsars Tower

10 The great gatehouse
11 The Swanne-tower
12 The houses in Clinton en

(below)   Radio Times Hulton Picture Library

Elizabeth' Regina.

2.PARALIPOM. 6.

was received into the inner Court with sweet musike. And so alighting from her horse, the drummes, fyfes and trumpets sounded: wherewith she mounted the stayres and went to her lodging."

The next day being Sunday, everyone went to church. "There was nothing done until the evening, at which time there were fireworks shewed upon the water, the which were both strange and well executed: as sometimes, passing under the water a long space, when all men had thought they had been quenched, they would rise and mount out of the water agayne and burn very furiously untill they were consumed."

Monday was hot, and the Queen did not go hunting until late in the day, returning by torch-light. On Tuesday there was music and dancing, and on Wednesday, hunting again. Thirteen bears were baited by dogs in the outer court on the Thursday, followed by more fireworks. And so it continued for another fortnight, with music and hunting, Italian acrobats and Latin speeches, and a play representing the massacre of the Danes in the year 1002.

After the Earl of Leicester's death in 1588, the year of the defeat of the Spanish Armada, Kenilworth Castle was claimed by the Crown, and eventually Robert Dudley's son sold it for a very low price (of which he never received a penny) and the castle became part of Queen Henrietta Maria's marriage-portion in 1626. During the Civil War it changed hands twice, without much fighting, but after the Battle of Edgehill it was held firmly by the Roundheads. After the

LEFT: *A water pageant staged for Queen Elizabeth I in 1591, from Nichol's* Progresses of Queen Elizabeth. *This particular pageant was at Elvetham (Hants); the Kenilworth pageant must have been somewhat similar.*

ABOVE: *Queen Elizabeth I at her devotions: a 1569 woodcut from Richard Day's* Christian Prayers and Meditations in English.

RIGHT: *Tudor ideas of ancient costume: a Dane and a Saxon as shown on the title-page of Speed's* Theatre of the Empire of Great Britain, *published in 1611.*

Cambridge University Library

On these pages and overleaf are four woodcuts from George Burberville's Booke of Hunting *and his* Booke of Falconrie, *both printed in 1575.* LEFT: *The Queen and her attendants stand on an elaborate wooden platform, raised to give a good view.* RIGHT: *The Queen at the kill; her attendants here wear the badge of the crowned Tudor rose, as they also do* (right) *where she is shown hawking.* OVERLEAF: *The picnic, or* "of the place where and howe an assembly should be made in the presence of a Prince or some honourable person".

that the Prince of their (if it so please them) doe alyght and take
assaye of the Deare with a sharpe knyfe, the whiche is done
L.ij,

35

ABOVE RIGHT: *The great Tudor doorway leading into the loggia from the pleasure garden on the north side of the castle; in the distance can be seen the door into the inner court. The Earl of Leicester had the loggia built within the forebuilding of the old Norman keep, whose inner entrance was above and to the left of the further archway.*

FAR RIGHT: *A panel of the timber framing of the walls of the Tudor stables, on the east side of the castle. The design is repeated many times (see overleaf).*

war, Parliament determined to destroy the castle but the Earl of Monmouth, who had managed to remain in occupation as the Queen's steward, successfully petitioned that it be *"slighted with as little spoil to the dwellinghouse as might be."* The 'slighting' was done by blowing up the outer (north) wall of the keep and breaching the outer wall and towers. But in 1650 the castle was sold, as royal property, to Colonel Hawkesworth (who had been in charge of the demolition work) and ten other Parliamentary officers. They broke down the dam, so draining the great lake and providing themselves with more than one hundred acres of rich farmland. Three hundred years later, and on the four hundredth anniversary of the accession of Queen Elizabeth I, the castle was given to the people of Kenilworth on 17th November, 1958.

OUTER COURT AND TILTYARD

The remaining buildings in the outer court, beyond the screen of trees, are a mixture of periods. The most prominent building is the long stables built for the Earl of Leicester in the sixteenth century. The ground floor has stone walls, but the upper storey is half-timbered and decorated with spiky cusped braces. The fine wooden roof is worth seeing from inside the barn, particularly all the beams and struts designed to prevent the roof from spreading and pushing outward the timber framing of the walls. In front of the barn are the foundations of another chapel, this one built for one of the fourteenth-century Earls of Lancaster: notice the three-sided east end, like the three-sided oriels of the inner court we have just left. The barn itself rests against part of the outer courtyard wall of the castle built in King John's reign, with two flanking towers on this side. That nearer the Tudor gatehouse (that is, to your left if you are looking at the barn) is the many-sided Lunn's Tower, with its little staircase turret. Although the tower was blown

ABOVE: *The Tudor stables built for the Earl of Leicester, with stone walls to the ground floor and brickwork and timber higher up. Notice the close-set timbers in the end wall (left), the chimney-stack and the small high windows.*

RIGHT: *The heavy roof covering the stables needed very strong framing to prevent its weight from forcing the walls outward. The roof trusses had no less than three horizontal tie-beams, with pairs of sloping braces, to hold the rafters in place.*

up in 1649, much of it still remains. On the outside it had an apron plinth at the base of the walls to resist attack, and also rows of arrow-slits at varying levels. The lowest parts of the cross-shaped arrow-slits are 'fish-tailed' to give a wider field of fire, exactly like those on the top floor of the keep. At the other end of the barn is the Water Tower, square in plan but with cut-off angles above the ground floor. This tower was designed more for comfort than defence, and has fine Early English windows and fireplaces. There was a similar building – the Swan or Swansnest Tower – on the opposite side of the castle, outside the Strong Tower, but very little remains of it now.

Returning to the main entrance, this was known as the Coltour or Mortimer's Tower. Originally it was little more than a passageway with side walls, but in the thirteenth century it was extended forwards and widened

with round-fronted towers on each side of the passage. Notice the vertical grooves for doors and portcullises at both ends of the gate passage.

The narrow causeway in front of Mortimer's Tower formed the barrage or dam of the great lake which surrounded the castle, with a lower pool below it. The causeway was known as the Tiltyard, and had side walls and a tower at each end. The outer tower is now in ruins; it was called the Gallery Tower, since it provided a grandstand from which to view the jousting in the Tilt-yard. A central fence ran down the middle of the Tiltyard, and two knights would ride towards each other with their lances at the ready, one on each side of the fence. It was probably here that the Great Tourney of Kenilworth took place in 1279, with more than a hundred knights and as many ladies, organized by Roger de Mortimer.

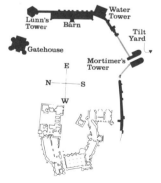

39

The modern bridge at the end of the causeway spans the site of an earlier bridge, which was made when the water level of the great lake was raised further in the thirteenth century. Beyond the bridge is the Brayes, an earth-work of bank and ditch which protected the outer end of the barrage and the lower pool. Today it surrounds the car park. Its outer wall and gate were merely a façade and not a proper defence-work, and the main purpose of the enclosure was for the holding of mêlées or mass tournaments. These were rough-and-tumble mass fights, rather like an uncontrolled Rugby scrum, in which valuable prizes – armour, horses and ransoms – were to be had by the victors. The knights' pavilions were probably pitched on the rim of the enclosure, near the projecting angles, facing the fighting-area in the middle. At the exit from the car park, there is one of these pavilion sites to the right; the mass of masonry on the left formed another dam, this time holding water in the moat surrounding the Brayes car park.

40

Armour of Robert Dudley, Earl of Leicester, 1564–88. This armour was made in the Royal Workshops at Greenwich in 1575 and is elaborately decorated with Dudley's emblem, the ragged staff.

OPPOSITE: *Tilting in the early sixteenth century. In this scene from the Westminster Tournament Roll (1511), Henry VIII breaks his lance on a Spaniard's helmet (just visible on the right, beyond the central fence separating the horses). Queen Catherine of Aragon, seated under a canopy, and others watch from a gallery alongside.*

LEFT: *Seventeenth-century fresco painting, formerly at Newnham Paddox, Monks Kirby (Warwickshire). Kenilworth Castle is seen from the east: Henry VIII's buildings are the low range in the centre, with a path leading to the door.*

RIGHT: *Lithograph (c.1839) of the castle, again from the east, after the disappearance of Henry VIII's range.*

OVERLEAF: *The castle from the great lake, looking north-east.* A. F. Kersting

BACK ENDPAPER: *General plan of Kenilworth, showing the extent of the great lake.*